Young Magician

CARD TRICKS

Oliver Ho

Illustrated by
Dave Garbot

Sterling Publishing Co., Inc.
New York

Dedication
For my brother and my parents

Library of Congress Cataloging-in-Publication Data

Ho, Oliver.
  Young magician. Card tricks / Oliver Ho.
          p. cm.
Includes index.
Summary: Provides step-by-step directions for performing simple magic tricks using cards.
  ISBN 1-4027-0045-8
  1. Card tricks–Juvenile literature. [1. Card tricks. 2. Magic tricks.] I. Title.
        GV1549 .H573 2003
        793.8'5–dc21

                                        2002008496

10 9 8 7 6 5 4 3 2 1

Published in paperback in 2005 by Sterling Publishing Co., Inc.
387 Park Avenue South, New York, NY 10016
© 2003 by Oliver Ho
Distributed in Canada by Sterling Publishing,
℅ Canadian Manda Group, 165 Dufferin Street,
Toronto, Ontario, Canada M6K 3H6
Distributed in Great Britain and Europe by Chris Lloyd at Orca Book
Services, Stanley House, Fleets Lane, Poole BH15 3AJ, England
Distributed in Australia by Capricorn Link (Australia) Pty. Ltd.
P.O. Box 704, Windsor, NSW 2756, Australia

Sterling ISBN 1-4027-0045-8 Hardcover
          ISBN 1-4027-2807-7 Paperback

For information about custom editions, special sales, premium and
corporate purchases, please contact Sterling Special Sales
Department at 800-805-5489 or specialsales@sterlingpub.com.

Contents

Card Lessons

All magicians know card tricks and if you want to become a magician, you'll need to learn a few. But before you start, you'll need some simple lessons about cards, like how to hold the cards, how to spread them, and how to cut and shuffle them. You will also need to know some "card words." These are the names of the different parts and marks on the cards.

Once you've gone through these card lessons, you can start learning the tricks. Make sure to ask an adult for help if any of the tricks are too hard. Always practice the tricks in front of a mirror so that you'll know how to do them perfectly. You can also try the tricks out in front of a friend who will promise to keep your magic secrets.

Important Card Words

Here are some words you'll need to know to do the tricks in this book.

Value: The value of a card can be a number (two to ten), an Ace (which equals one), or a court card (Jack, Queen, or King—a Jack equals eleven, a Queen equals twelve, and a King equals thirteen).

Suit: A card can be one of four suits: Clubs, Hearts, Diamonds, and Spades.

Face: The face of a card is the side that shows its value and suit.

Back: The back of a card is the side with the pattern on it. It's the side that doesn't show the value of the card.

Faceup: To have a card faceup is to show the face of the card.

Facedown: To have a card facedown is to show the back of the card.

Deck: A deck is what you have when all the cards are stacked one on top of the other.

Edges: When you look at a card or at the deck, there are four edges: the top edge, the bottom edge, the left edge, and the right edge. The top and bottom edges are also called the short edges. The left and right edges are also called the long edges.

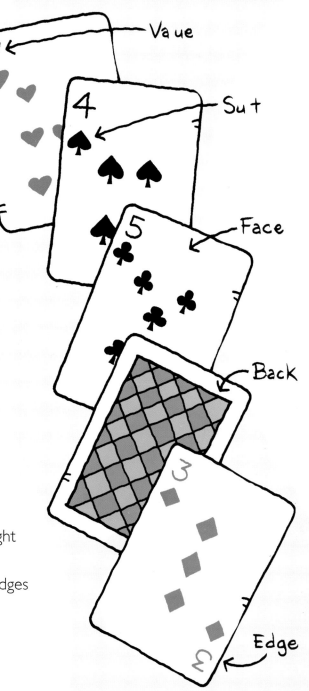

Va ue

Su t

Face

Back

Edge

Finding the Right Deck

When you do card tricks, you need a deck that fits in your hand. You should start with a child's size deck when you are learning the card tricks.

How to Hold the Deck

Hold the deck facedown in your left hand. Place your first finger around the short edge, like in this picture.

Now you're holding the deck like a real magician. This is called the magician's grip.

How to Square the Deck

To square up the cards, you just straighten up the deck so that all the edges are even.

Before Squaring...

After Squaring

How to Spread the Cards

When you ask someone to "pick a card," this is the best way to spread the cards out for him: Hold the deck in your left hand and push some of the cards over to your right hand, like in these pictures below.

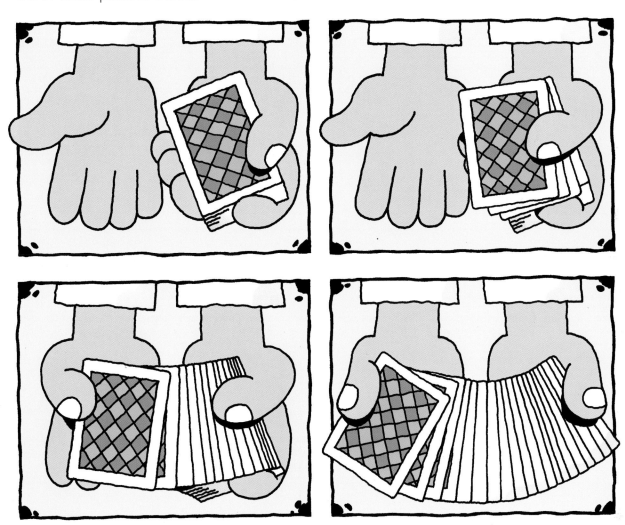

How to Cut the Cards

To cut the cards means you take the top half of the deck and move it to the bottom. You can do this in your hands or on the table.

To cut the deck in your hands, hold the deck in your left hand and follow the pictures.

To cut the deck on the table, place the deck on the table and follow the pictures below. Make sure you square up the deck after cutting the cards.

How to Shuffle

Shuffling the cards is an easy way to mix them all up without making a mess. One of the easiest ways is called the overhand shuffle.

1. Hold the deck in your left hand.

2. Take some cards from the bottom with your right hand.

3. Pull some cards from your right hand into your left a few times.

4. When all the cards are back in your left hand, square up the deck.

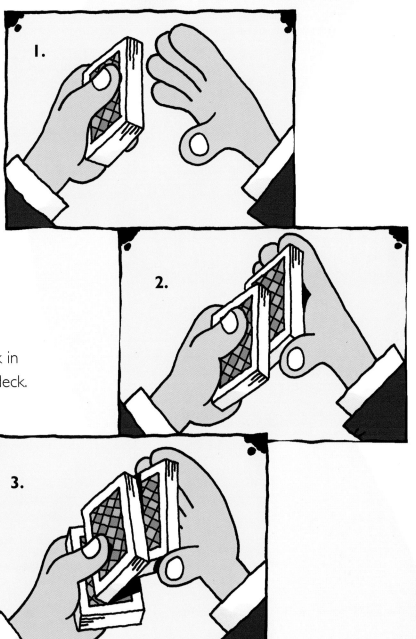

9

The Rising Card

The Magic

A card floats out of a deck you're holding!

The Trick

1. Hold the deck up in your right hand so that your audience can see the card on the bottom of the deck.

2. Tap the top edge of the deck with the first finger of your left hand. When your finger touches the deck, secretly stick out

the little finger of your left hand and use it to push the top card partway up. Make sure to do this slowly. If you wiggle your little finger when you push the card up, the card will look even more like it's floating.

Amazing Aces

The Magic

After you put the two black Aces and the Ace of Diamonds in different parts of the deck, they show up together in the middle of the deck, and the Ace of Diamonds has been turned over.

Before You Start

Take all the Aces out of the deck. Then take the Ace of Diamonds and turn it over so that it's the only card that's faceup. Put it on the bottom of the deck.

The Trick

1. Hold the two black Aces in front of the Ace of Hearts. Spread the two black Aces apart so you can see just the tip of the heart behind them, like in the picture. This creates an optical illusion. The tip of the heart looks like the top part of the diamond.

2. Show the three cards like this to the audience. Tell them you have the Ace of Clubs, the Ace of Spades, and the Ace of Diamonds. Then square up the cards and put them facedown on top of the deck.

3. Take the top card, call it the Ace of Diamonds, but make sure that no one sees that it's really the Ace of Hearts. Stick the card into the middle of the deck.

4. Take the new top card, show it to the audience, and put it on the bottom of the deck. Make sure that no one sees the Ace of Diamonds, which is hidden and turned over on the bottom of the deck.

Ace of Diamonds is faceup on the bottom of the deck

Black Ace

5. Turn the top card over to show the audience, then put it back on top of the deck. Tell your audience that you put the Ace of Diamonds in the middle of the deck. Then you put one of the black Aces on the bottom of the deck and the last one is on top of the deck.

6. Cut the deck. You can cut it a few times, if you like. Make a magical pass over it and then spread the cards to show the Ace of Diamonds turned faceup in the middle of the deck.

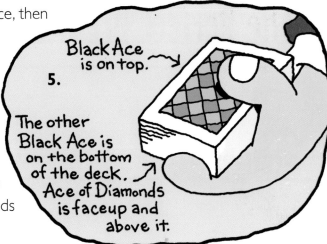

Black Ace is on top.

5.

The other Black Ace is on the bottom of the deck. Ace of Diamonds is faceup and above it.

6.

7. Take out the Ace of Diamonds and the two cards just below it. Turn them over to show the two black Aces.

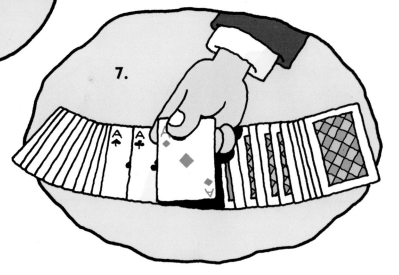

7.

The Perfect Prediction

The Magic

You put out three cards and ask someone in your audience to choose one. When she does, you show a piece of paper that says she would choose that card!

What You'll Need

Three slips of paper   *A pen*

Before You Start

Take any three cards from the deck. For example, let's say you use the Two of Clubs, the Ten of Diamonds, and the Queen of Hearts.

Set out the three slips of paper.

On one slip of paper write, "You will choose the Two of Clubs."

On the second piece of paper write, "You will choose the Ten of Diamonds."

On the third write, "You will choose the Queen of Hearts."

Now here's the real secret: Hide each of these pieces of paper in a different place. For example, you can put one of them in your left pocket, one in your right pocket, and one in your back pocket. Make sure you remember which pocket each note is in.

You can also hide the pieces of paper in much stranger places, such as in each of your shoes, under a chair that your audience is sitting on, or taped to the bottom of the table. Use your imagination to find three places to hide the papers, but be sure to remember where you hid each one.

Put your three cards on top of the deck. Make sure you know what order they are in.

The Trick

1. Deal out the top three cards so that they are facedown on the table. Ask someone from your audience to point to one of them.
2. As soon as she points to one, you know which card she's chosen. Tell her to wait before she turns it over. Take out the piece of paper with that card written on it.
3. Tell her that you knew which card she would choose.
4. Turn the piece of paper over at the same time she turns her card over. Show her that the card matches what you wrote on the paper.

The Key Card Method

The most popular card tricks are "pick a card" tricks. You ask someone to choose a card. You can't see what card she chose but you find it in some magical way.

One of the easiest ways to do these tricks is to use a secret that magicians call the "key card" method. Once you know this secret, there are a lot of different ways you can use it.

1. Spread out the cards and have someone from your audience take a card from the deck.

2. While she's looking at her card, turn around. Tell your audience you're turning around so you can't see her card. But what you're really doing is looking at the card on the bottom of the deck. Remember this card. It's your key card for this trick.

3. Turn back and ask your friend to put her card on top of the deck. You can also put the deck on the table and ask her to put her card on top of it.

4. Cut the deck (or ask her to do it). This will put your key card next to hers. You can cut the deck as many times as you want, but make sure you do not shuffle it. That would move the key card away from her card.

5. Look through the deck. When you see your key card, her card will be to the right of it.

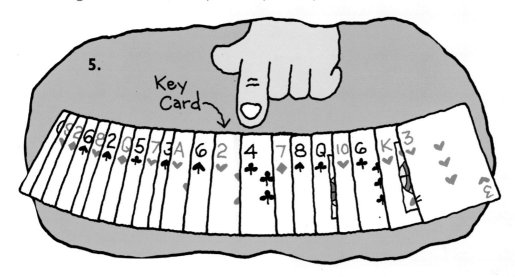

6. Take her card out from the deck and show it to her and the audience.

Now there are a lot more "magical" ways to show her card. We'll show you six different ways over the next few pages.

Fingerprints

The Magic

You find a card that someone from your audience chose by studying the cards for fingerprints.

The Trick

1. Following the key card method (see pages 16–17), ask someone from your audience to choose a card.

2. After you or your friend has cut the deck a few times, leave it on the table. Then ask to see your friend's hand. Tell him that you're studying his fingerprints.

3. Pick up the deck and hold it facedown. Deal the cards one at a time onto the table. Turn each card faceup before you place it on the table. Pretend to study each card for fingerprints before you place it on the table.

4. Once you get to your key card, the very next one you deal will be your friend's chosen card. When you turn his card faceup, pretend to study it, and tell him that you found his fingerprints.

←Friend's Card

←Key Card

The Next Card

The Magic

Someone from your audience chooses a card and hides it in the deck. You deal the cards one at a time on the table. When you get to her card, you promise your friend that the next card you turn over will be hers. She thinks you're wrong, but you show the card and it's hers!

The Trick

1. Following the key card method (see pages 16–17), ask someone from your audience to choose a card. Then cut the deck a few times.

2. Hold the deck facedown. Deal out the cards one at a time. Turn each card faceup before placing it down on the table.

3. Once you see your key card, you know the next one will be your friend's chosen card.

4. Deal out your friend's card and pretend you don't know that it's hers. Deal out a few more cards on top of her chosen card.

5. Tell your friend that the next card you turn over will be hers. But because she has already seen her card, she will think you're wrong.

6. Instead of dealing the next card, look through the cards you've already turned over. Find the card that you know is your friend's. Turn it facedown and then turn it faceup. Just like you promised, the next card you turned over is hers!

Lifting Weights

The Magic

You find your friend's card by weighing it in your hand. It is more "magically" heavy than the other cards.

The Trick

1. Use the key card method to place your friend's chosen card next to the one that you know (see pages 16–17). Hold the deck facedown. Then start turning the cards faceup one at a time.

2. Pretend to weigh each card in your hand before you drop the card on the table. Tell your friend that he added magic to his card when he chose it. The magic makes his card weigh more, but only a magician can feel the added weight.

3. When you turn over your key card, you'll know that the very next card will be your friend's. Pretend that his card feels heavier. Tell him this must be his card.

Mind Reader

The Magic

You find your friend's card by reading her mind!

The Trick

1. Following the key card method (see pages 16–17), ask your friend to choose a card. Cut the deck and place it facedown on the table.

2. Tell your friend to think about what's on her card because you will try to read her mind.

3. Pretend to be thinking hard and then act as if you're starting to see something.

4. Turn the deck faceup on the table and spread the cards to the right. Look for your key card. When you find it, take out the card to the right of it. This will be your friend's card.

Key Card ⟶ ⟵ Friend's Card

Inside Out

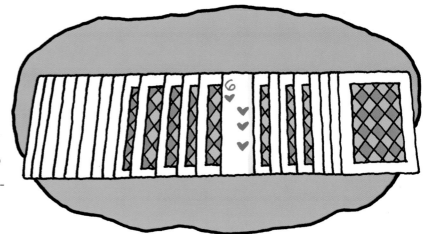

The Magic

Someone from your audience chooses a card and it ends up being the only card that's face-up in the deck.

The Trick

1. Following the key card method (see pages 16–17), ask someone from your audience to choose a card. Cut the deck a few times.

2. Look through the deck. Tell your friend that you're trying to find his card.

3. When you find your key card, cut the deck so that the key card is on the bottom of the deck.

3.

Friend's Card on the top

Key Card on the bottom

4. Your friend's card should be the top card on the deck. Square up the cards and tell your audience that you're having trouble finding your friend's card.

5. Hold the deck behind your back.

6. Tell the audience that you're going to try to find your friend's card without looking at the deck.

7. Take the top card (your friend's card) and turn it over. Stick it in the middle of the deck. Square up the cards.

8. Ask your friend to name his card. Then spread out the cards facedown on the table. His card will be the only one that's faceup.

Inside Out Again

The Magic

Here's another way to do the last trick:
Someone from your audience chooses
a card. That card magically turns
faceup in the deck.

Before You Start

Hold the deck facedown. Turn
the bottom card over so that
it is faceup. Now you're ready
to begin.

The Trick

1. Spread out the cards and ask someone in the audience to pick a card. Make sure no
one can see that the bottom card is faceup.

2. After your friend chooses a card, turn away from her and ask her to show the card to
everyone.

3. While you're turned away, secretly turn the deck over in your hand. The deck is now faceup but it looks facedown because your bottom card is on top.

4. Turn around. The audience will believe the entire deck is still facedown. Take your friend's facedown card. Without looking at it, stick her card into the deck.

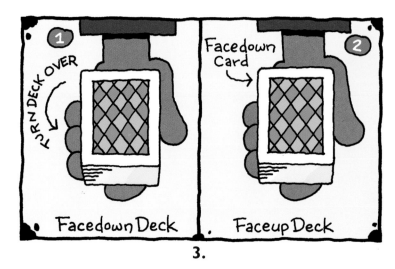

TURN DECK OVER

1

Facedown Deck

Facedown Card

2

Faceup Deck

3.

5. Hold the deck behind your back and tell your audience that you'll try to find her card. What you're really doing is turning the bottom card faceup.

6. Spread the cards facedown on the table. Her card will be the only one in the deck that's faceup.

Turn bottom card faceup behind your back

5.

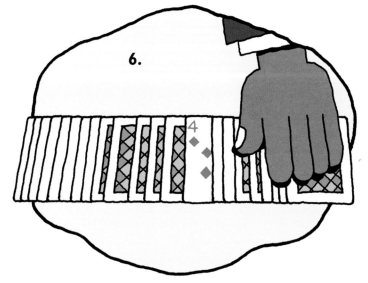

6.

The One-way Deck

The Magic

Someone in your audience picks a card from the deck. You turn around while she shows the audience her card. She puts the card back into the deck. You can tell which card she picked.

Get a One-way Deck

The secret to this trick is the type of deck you use. Look at the pictures on the back of different decks. Some decks have a pattern on the back that looks the same whether the cards are right-side up or upside down. Other decks

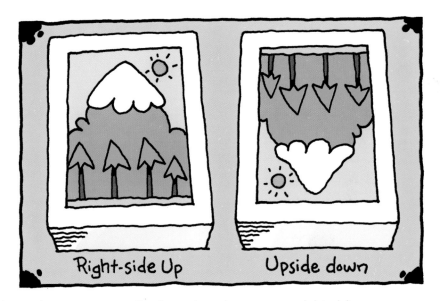

Right-side Up   Upside down

have pictures on the back so that you can tell when the pictures are right-side up or upside down. Magicians call these "one-way decks."

Before You Start

Turn all cards so the pictures on the back are right-side up.

The Trick

1. Spread the cards out for your friend to choose a card. After she picks her card, turn away with the rest of the deck in your hand. Tell her that you don't want to see the card.

2. What you're really doing is turning the deck around so that when she puts her card back into the deck, it will be the only one where the picture on the back is upside down.

3. Turn back to face her and ask her to put the card back into the deck. Make sure that her card will be the only one with the upside-down picture on its back. If it isn't, ask her to show everyone the card once more. Turn the deck around while she is doing this.

3.

4. Once her card is in the deck, you can shuffle and cut it as many times as you wish. Her card will be easy to find. You only need to look at the backs of the cards and pick out the one where the picture on the back is turned over.

5. As you did with the "key card tricks" (see pages 18–26), you can show your friend's card in a lot of different ways:

✦ You could just pull it from the deck.

✦ Cut the cards so hers is on top and deal it out to her.

✦ Cut the cards so hers is on the bottom. As you square up the cards, secretly look at her card. Cut the deck again so that she doesn't see her card. Then pretend to read her mind.

Use your imagination to come up with more ways to show her card.

The Four Thieves, Part 1

The Magic

While telling a story about four robbers, you show everyone the four Jacks and then place them into four different parts of the deck. When you give the top of the deck a magical touch, all four Jacks show up together there.

Before You Start

Take the four Jacks and three other cards out of the deck. Hold the four Jacks so that they face you.

Put the three other cards behind the last Jack. If you turn this packet of cards face-down, the three cards are on top and the four Jacks are below them.

Take a King out of the deck, and leave it faceup on the table.

4 Jacks are on the bottom.

The Trick

1. Hold the packet of seven cards. Leave the deck facedown on the table. Spread out the four Jacks so that everyone can see them.

2. Make sure that you don't show the three cards hidden behind the last Jack. Your audience should believe you're only holding four Jacks.

Three cards hiding behind last Jack.

2.

3. Tell your audience that you will be using these four Jacks to tell a story. They are four thieves who want to rob a building.

4. Square up the packet and place it facedown on top of the rest of the deck. Tilt your hand down a little so that your audience is looking at the back of the deck instead of the edge of it.

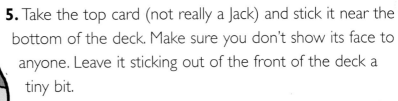

4.

5. Take the top card (not really a Jack) and stick it near the bottom of the deck. Make sure you don't show its face to anyone. Leave it sticking out of the front of the deck a tiny bit.

6. Tell your audience that the first thief went to the first floor.

7. Take the next card (not a Jack) from the top of the deck and stick it into the middle of the deck. Again, make sure not to show its face. Leave it sticking out a little bit.

8. Tell your audience that the second thief went to the second floor.

9. Take the next card from the top (not a Jack). Without showing its face, stick it close to the top of the deck. Leave it sticking out a little like the others.

10. Tell your audience that the third robber went to the third floor.

11. Turn over the top card and show everyone that it's a Jack. Turn it facedown and stick it into the deck about one or two cards from the top. Leave it sticking out like the others.

12. Tell your audience the fourth robber went to the fourth floor, which was near the roof.

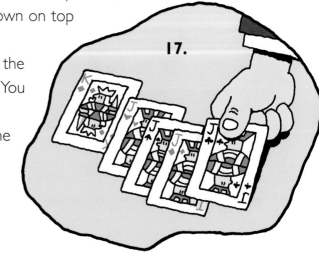

3 extra cards

4 Jacks still on top.

12.

13. Slowly square up the deck. Push in the four cards. Make sure no one can see the faces of the cards that are sticking out. Place the deck facedown on the table.

14. Tell your audience that just as the thieves were looking around, an alarm went off. Tap the top of the deck and make a sound like a ringing bell.

15. Take the King that you left on the table and tell your audience that this is a police officer. Put it facedown on top of the deck.

King

15.

16. Deal out the top five cards. You should have the King followed by the four Jacks.

17.

17. Tell your audience that the police officer chased all four thieves to the roof and caught them.

The Four Thieves, Part 2

The Magic

This is another way of doing the last trick. You put the four Jacks at different places in the deck. You cut the cards once and then all the Jacks come together.

This trick is a little easier to do than the last trick. You don't have to hide as many cards in your hand and you can show more of the Jacks to the audience during the trick.

Before You Start

Take out the four Jacks, two other cards, and a King. Leave the King faceup on the table. Hold the four Jacks. Place the two other cards behind the third Jack.

Two other cards hidden behind Jack number 3.

The Trick

1. Show the four Jacks to the audience. Make sure no one sees the two other cards hidden in them. Square up the cards and place them facedown on top of the rest of the deck.
2. Take the top card (a Jack) and show it to the audience. Then place it on the bottom of the deck. Tell them the first thief waited on the first floor.

3. Take the next card (not a Jack). Don't show this card to the audience. Stick it near the bottom of the deck. Tell your audience that the second thief went to the second floor.

4. Take the card (not a Jack). Again, don't show this card to the audience. Stick it near the middle of the deck. Tell your audience that the third thief went to the third floor.

5. Turn over the top card (a Jack). Tell your audience the last thief waited on the roof.

6. Place the King facedown on top of the deck. Tell your audience this King is a police officer and a magician. Cut the deck.

7. Turn the deck faceup and spread the cards. The King will be between the four Jacks.

8. Tell your audience that the magic police officer caught all four thieves.

7.

Messy Shuffle

The Magic

You mix the deck so that some cards are faceup and others are facedown. By making one magic cut, you bring them all facing one way.

The Trick

1. Hold the deck facedown in your left hand. Take a small bunch of cards from the top into your right hand.

2. Turn the cards in your right hand faceup and put them on top of the cards in your left hand.

2.

3. Take all the faceup cards and a bunch of facedown cards into your right hand. Turn these over and place them back onto the deck. Keep doing this until you've gone through the entire deck.

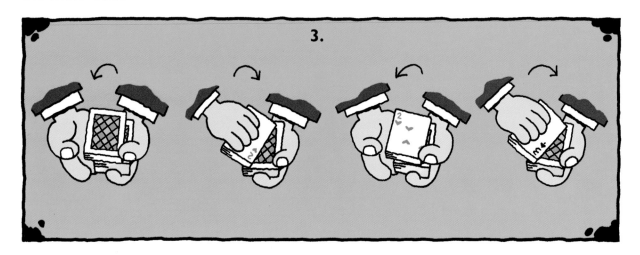

4. It looks as though the deck is completely mixed up with faceup and facedown cards. But the deck is really divided into two halves. Their backs are just facing each other.

5. Find the place where the two halves meet and separate them. Turn one half over and shuffle them together.

6. Now you can spread the cards to show that they're all facing one way!

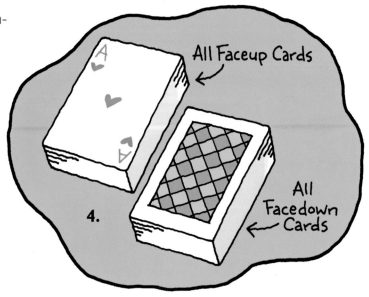

All Faceup Cards

All Facedown Cards

4.

Divided Deck, Part 1

The Magic

You cut the deck into two piles. Someone from your audience chooses a card from the first pile and places it into the second pile. You shuffle the second pile and then find his card right away.

Before You Start

You need to divide the deck into two groups. One group should have all the red cards (all the Hearts and Diamonds). The other group should have all the black cards (all the Clubs and Spades).

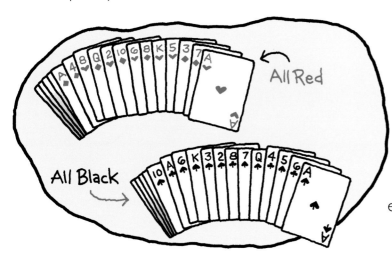

All Red

All Black

The Trick

1. Hold the deck so that it faces you. Divide the deck in half so that you have one deck that has all the red cards and another one that has all the black cards. Place each deck facedown on the table.

4.

Deck 2

2. Your audience should believe that you've just cut the deck. They don't know that you've divided the red and black cards.

3. Ask someone from your audience to point to one pile. Whichever pile he chooses, spread those cards from that pile so that they are facedown on the table. Ask him to pick a card. After he takes one, square up the pile that the card came from and put it away.

4. Ask him to show everyone the card. Then tell him to put the card facedown into the second pile of cards on the table.

5. Pick up the second pile of cards and shuffle it as many times as you wish. Turn the cards so they face you. Ask your audience to think of his card.

6. Look through the cards for the one card that is a different color from the others.

7. Take his card out and place it faceup on the table. Shuffle the two halves of the deck back together so no one will discover your secret.

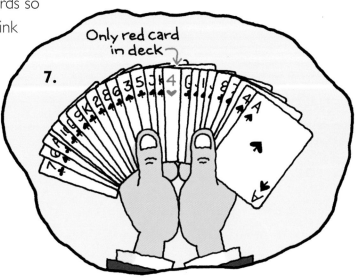

Only red card in deck

7.

Divided Deck, Part 2

The Magic

Here is another way to do the last trick: You divide the deck in half. Someone from your audience chooses a card from the first pile and places it into the second pile. After shuffling the second pile, you can find her card right away.

Before You Start

In the last trick, you divided the deck into reds and blacks. The only problem with that trick is that if your friend turns over any of the decks, she will know your secret. The way we do this trick is a little safer.

Hearts & Clubs

Diamonds & Spades

Instead of dividing the deck into reds and blacks, this time divide it into four suits (Hearts, Clubs, Diamonds and Spades). Make sure one half of the deck has all the Hearts and Clubs. Make sure the other deck has all the Diamonds and Spades.

The Trick

1. Hold the deck so it that faces you. Divide the deck so that all the Hearts and Clubs are in one deck and the Diamonds and Spades are in another deck. Place each deck facedown on the table.

2. Ask someone from your audience to point to one pile. Whichever pile she chooses, spread those cards from that pile so that they are facedown on the table. Ask her to pick a card. After she takes one, square up the pile that the card came from and put it away.

3. Ask her to show everyone the card. Then tell her to put the card facedown into the second pile of cards on the table.

4. Pick up the second pile of cards and shuffle it as many times as you wish. Turn the cards so they face you. Ask your friend to think of her card.

5. Look through the cards for the one that has a different suit than the others. In the deck that has only Hearts and Clubs, look for the Diamond or Spade. In the deck that has only Diamonds and Spades, look for the Heart or Club. Take out that card and place it faceup on the table.

Only Diamond in the deck

5.

6. You can repeat this trick, if you like. If people accidentally look through the cards, they probably won't notice that the two piles are divided into suits.

Two-card Prediction

The Magic

You pull out two cards from the deck and place them facedown on the table. Then you ask someone from the audience to cut the deck. The two cards that he chooses have the same numbers and colors as the two cards you pulled out.

The Trick

1. Shuffle the deck. Tell your audience you're going to choose two cards that will be the same number and color that anyone from the audience will pick later.

2. Look through the cards. Pretend to be thinking hard. What you're really doing is looking at the top and bottom cards.

3. Pick out two cards that match the top and bottom cards' number and color. For example, if the top card is the Three of Clubs and the bottom card is the Six of Diamonds, you pick out the Three of Spades and the Six of Hearts.

4. Place your two cards facedown on the table.

5. Put the deck facedown on the table and ask someone from your audience to cut the deck into two piles. Pick up the bottom half and place it on top of the other half, but place it sideways across the deck so that the cards look like a plus sign.

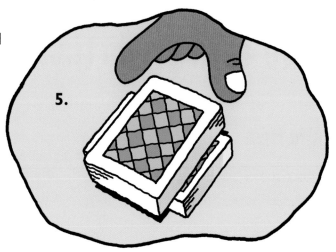

6. Go over the trick so far with your audience. Tell them that you shuffled the deck and took out two cards. Then you had your friend cut the deck anywhere he wanted. By talking like this, you're making your audience forget which half of the deck was the original top half and which half was the original bottom half.

7. Pick up the top half of the deck. Turn it faceup and place it on the table. Then turn over the top card of the other half.

8. Turn over the two cards that you placed facedown on the table. They will match the numbers and colors of the two faceup cards on the deck.

Dealing the Aces

The Magic

You show four Aces and put them on top of the deck. You deal the top four cards to yourself and the next four to your audience. When all the cards are turned over, your audience has the Aces.

Before You Start

Take out the four Aces and four other cards. Put all the Aces facedown in one pile. Put the four other cards facedown on top of them. Pick up these cards and turn the pack faceup. You're ready to start.

4 Other Cards behind the 4 Aces.

The Trick

1. Spread out the four Aces so your audience can see them. Make sure you don't show the four other cards. They should be hiding behind the last Ace.

2. Square up the packet, turn it facedown. Place it on top of the deck.

3. Deal the first four cards (which are not the Aces) facedown to yourself. Deal the next four cards (which are the Aces) facedown to your audience. Your audience will believe that you have the four Aces.

4. Make a magical pass over all the cards. Turn them over and show that your audience has the four Aces.

Four other cards hidden behind

1.

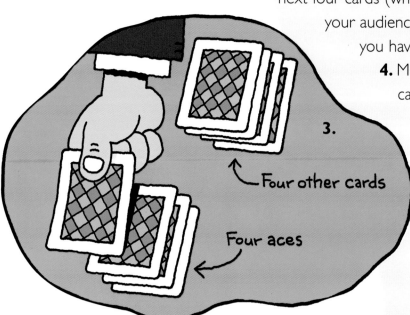

3.

Four other cards

Four aces

Royal Party

The Magic

You use some cards to tell a story about four royal families that had a big party. All the families were together, then they became mixed up in a storm. Magically, you show all the men, women, and children from each family together.

The Trick

1. Take out all the face cards (the Kings, Queens, Jacks) and all the Aces. Put away the rest of the deck.

2. Deal out the four Kings faceup. Tell your audience that four Kings were having a party.

3. Deal out the four Queens faceup. Place one Queen on top of each King. Make sure the suits match.

4. Tell your audience that the Kings invited their Queens.

5. Deal out the four Jacks faceup. Place one Jack on top of each Queen. Again, make sure that the suits match.

6. Tell your audience that the royal couples invited their sons.

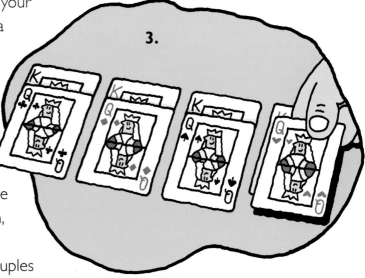

7. Tell your audience that a storm came, so everyone locked himself into his rooms.

8. Deal out the four Aces faceup. Place one Ace on top of each Jack. Make sure that the suits match.

9. Tell your audience to pretend that the Aces are the locks on the doors.

10. Square up each pile. Place one pile on top of the other pile until you make a small deck. Turn the deck facedown.

11. You can cut this packet as many times as you like. You can also ask someone in your audience to cut the packet. Make sure you don't shuffle the packet—only keep cutting it.

12. Tell your audience that the storm scared everyone. It shook the castle and rattled the locks on the doors.

13. Deal out four cards facedown. Deal them out from the top of the deck and have the cards go from left to right.

14. After you deal out the fourth card, deal out another four cards on top of these. Remember to deal from the left to the right. Keep dealing out the cards this way until you have four piles of cards.

15. Tell your audience that it was a magic storm. When it was over, all the Kings were together in one room, all the Queens in another, all the Jacks in another, and all the locks in another.

16. Turn each pile face up. There will be one pile of Kings, one of Queens, one of Jacks, and one of Aces.

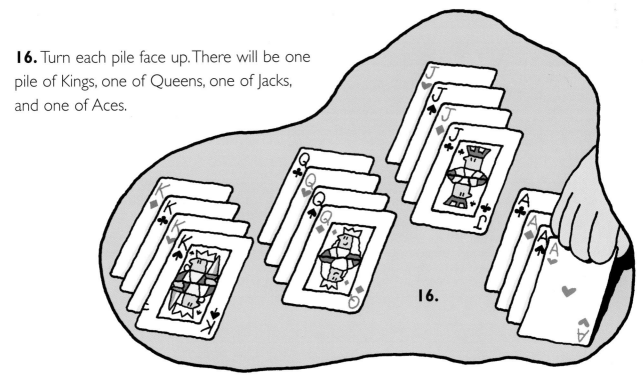

Index